You is for Unique

Women's feelings about body image
and self-esteem

JULIA HAGUE

**Grosvenor House
Publishing Limited**

Julia Hague is hereby identified as author of this
work in accordance with Section 77 of the Copyright, Designs
and Patents Act 1988

The book cover picture is copyright to Julia Hague

This book is published by
Grosvenor House Publishing Ltd
28-30 High Street, Guildford, Surrey, GU1 3HY.
www.grosvenorhousepublishing.co.uk

A CIP record for this book
is available from the British Library

ISBN 978-1-907211-00-3

Table of Contents

Preface	vii
Acknowledgements	ix
You Is For Unique	1
So Lovely	7
Pivot	11
Booby Prize	18
Nice Things Come In Small Packages	24
Bountifully Bootylicious	29
Distortion	34
Beauty Secret	40
Unbeliever	44
Net Worth	48
Reality TV	52
Her Suit	57
Upset Tummy	66
Wasted	70
Reach Inside	75
Mirror, Mirror	83
Elation	88
Tube Lines	94
Reflections	99
About The Author & Credits	102-103

Preface

We've all been almost programmed in one way or another to believe that what we see reflected in the media, in whatever form that takes, be it television, films or magazines, is the way women, or men even, should look. For women, attractive means only being slim, perfectly featured and having all the right attributes. Why should a person look one way or another, be a particular size or shape, or follow rules that were man made?

Interestingly that image, which has always been portrayed, never seems to reflect you and me and what we really look like. Or for that matter what women we see every day in the street look like. Why is that? It seems bizarre when each and every one of us is unique, and sadly that uniqueness, that diversity of size, shape, age and what makes someone attractive is not acknowledged. So an enormous proportion of women grow up to feel unworthy, less attractive, less important than anyone we see portrayed in the media because they don't fit the "rules" which the media has made up about what we should look like. Perfection rules ok. And yet it doesn't. And it shouldn't.

I have talked to many, many women who have shared their stories and their feelings about body image and self esteem. Some told me for the first time about how they felt, what they had done to themselves as a result of feeling ashamed of their bodies, of having lost their sense of personal self worth and how they had lost their sense of wonder at who they were. Some were courageous in sharing, others relieved to have someone who finally understood. I drew from their experiences; their feelings and I drew from my own experiences and feelings. I then shut myself away night after night for about eight months and literally became eighteen different women, and told their stories as a series of written monologues.

A selection of these monologues was adapted for the stage show "Me So Lovely", performed in Toronto for charity in the hot summer of 2008 by an array of beautiful actresses of all shapes, sizes, and ages. The show was crewed by a group of volunteers who flew in from all over the world, and was directed and produced by the talented team from MSL Productions Inc, a company formed specifically to bring the monologues to the stage that summer.

But all the pieces had always cried out to be in print, and I owed it to the women who had shared their stories with me to get that done, to enable more women to read them and immerse themselves in other women's worlds and realise that any feelings they had about themselves were felt by hundreds of thousands of others, and that they were not alone.

So here you have them in your hands. Women's innermost thoughts and feelings which will take you on a roller coaster ride of emotions, from laughter to tears, and which will, hopefully, leave you at the end realising that you are not alone.
In fact you are in a majority, and yet you are unique.

Acknowledgements

I doubt that words can sufficiently express my thanks and love for those people who have supported me writing these pieces, loved them and then encouraged me to get them published so that others could also delve into the pages and learn about themselves and about those who are around them.

My dear, much-loved, patient and caring husband Peter, without your support these words would not be in print. My beautiful daughter, Rebecca who shared her own feelings about body image and self-esteem with me, I love you. My ever supportive mother Elise and twin brother Philip, thank you. To these wonderful family members I give my love and grateful thanks for enduring the endless months and months of losing me to the keyboard and to the telephone conversations, and for telling me I could do it.

My friends, without whose encouragement and love the words in this book would have been an idea languishing on the dusty bookshelf in my mind, and not sitting in your hands right now. There are so many, but I'd like to say especially to Jennifer Scheffler, Liesl Bland, Becky Preen, Kay Jacobs, Jaclyn MacRae, Fiona Donovan, Mari King and Sue Sampson that your ongoing support and belief in me throughout the years of this endeavour means so much to me. Thank you probably isn't enough, but you know how I feel about you all, and that's all that matters.

Frances Gumley-Mason – the best employer in the world and a good friend. Thank you for encouraging me to be what I need to be and allowing me the time and space to do what I do.

And for four very special friends who never gave up on me, believed in me and held me up. Friends who made sure I never gave up on myself.

Amanda Tapping – my dear and wonderful friend. Thank you for never letting me give up. For understanding me as only a true friend can, and always having words of advice for me. For the faith which you've always shown in me and for not only believing in me, but believing in what I was doing and encouraging me to take a chance and fly and holding my hand while I made the attempt. Your true friendship, love and encouragement are the rock on which this book sits.

Tracy North – you're a star and best friend. Thank you for enthusiastically embracing the original concept back in early 2007 and letting me talk to you for hours on end about it. For helping with the design of my book cover. For listening to me, crying with me, laughing with me, not always agreeing with me, and just simply being there for me, always.

Sue George – my proof-reader and dear friend. Thank you for being the eternal rally cry I needed, the sounding board and the voice of sanity. For your faith and dogged determination that the pieces would make it into print, merci.

Damien Walshe – for talking things through with me, advising me, believing in me and encouraging me through the ups and downs of writing this book. I couldn't have done this without your support and friendship.

To all the women who I have talked to about body image and self esteem. To those who shared their stories willingly. To those who spoke tentatively, nervously and sometimes even eagerly; some for the first time in their lives. For all of you who entrusted me to tell other women about your feelings and experiences through this book, thank you. I am humbled by what you told me and what you shared, and I am deeply moved by those who told me that I have, in some way, changed their lives. I hope I've done you all justice.

A huge thank you to Alexandra Allen who drew the front cover image and Beryl Maw who photographed it and facilitated the logo. I am eternally grateful to you both for your talent and for your help.

Lastly, to Grosvenor House Publishers, my grateful thanks for your vision in enabling authors to have the opportunity to believe in their work and giving them the independence to achieve their goals.

—〜〜—

The author will donate £1.00 for every book sold to Sanctuary for Kids - Amanda Tapping's charity initiative to help channel funds to small charities throughout the world.

You can contact the author and find out more about this charity at www.youisforunique.com

You Is For Unique

Let me tell you a fact.
There are millions of women around the world locked in a constant battle.
A self-berating, self-destroying war.
A war which is of their own making.
And yet they don't realise it.
Don't realise that in order to win, they merely have to change the way they think.

And accept.
That in their hands, in their minds, lies a truth.
A truth which is being hidden from them by others.
Their lives have been controlled.
From the day they were old enough to read magazines, and watch television.
Despite what their mothers told them.
And impressed upon them.
That they were beautiful.
They were suddenly told that they weren't good enough.
That their beauty didn't exist.
Couldn't exist.
Because someone else had made the rules.
Rules about what beauty equals.
That if they don't fit into a set mould, they have somehow failed.

And as a result women (and men) are being judgemental.
On themselves. As well as others.
Judging that because someone else's version of beauty doesn't match what they see in the mirror, that somehow the failure to conform has tainted their lives.

And as a result.
A result of someone else's view.
Someone else's thoughts.
They are being unkind.
Unkind to themselves.
Unkind to others.
Denying the beauty which is in them.
Which has always been within them.
The beauty which lasts a lifetime.
The beauty which they can embrace and rejoice in.
The beauty which is simple.
Wonderful.
Unique.

More precious than anything they own materially.
The beauty which truly belongs to them and no one else.
Which they have power over. And no one else does.
The beauty which, if they accept it, will enhance how they feel
about others too.
And it is a beauty which will last forever.

It is their own beauty.
The beauty they have right now.
Without change.
Without enhancement.
Those women can finish the war right now.
This minute.
This second.
It's that easy.
So can you.

You don't believe me, do you?
I can see the scepticism in your eyes.
The doubt written all over your face.

Well, just take your own hand.
Hold it gently and stroke it. Feel the skin. The texture.
See the colour. Every line. Every freckle. Every imperfection.
The fingers. The nails.
Turn it over and trace a finger lightly across the palm.
The simplicity which is your hand is more complex than you think.
It is beautiful. Stunning. A miracle.
Let your eyes linger over it and feel its strength.
Love it.

Imagine if you were to look at every part of your body and feel the same!
You should.
You can.
Next time you look in a mirror choose a part of your body you feel good about and do the same.
Rejoice in it.

Then choose a part of your body you loathe. (Even though you shouldn't loathe it at all)
You avoid looking at.
Because you believe it to be imperfect.
Look at it with new eyes.
Take ownership of it.
Take responsibility for it.
You will find it's not so unattractive after all.
Find something lovely about it. The skin. The colour. The shape.
Anything.
You **will** find something.

Your body.
It's yours. You can't disown it.
Can't throw it away.
Can't give it back.
Can't part exchange it.

Why should you?
Why should you let someone else tell you who you should be?
How you should look?
How you should dress?
How you should feel about yourself?
How can someone else rule your life so much?
They shouldn't rule it at all.

Go ahead.
Embrace yourself.
Love yourself.
The body which you were born with is unique.
Beautiful.
Fabulous.
It belongs to you.
It belongs to no one else.
You are responsible for it.

No one has the right to tell you how you should feel about it.
No one can take it away from you.
No matter how poor you are, how depressed you are, wherever you
are in the world.
There is one constant.
You. Your body.
It goes everywhere with you.

It's reliable.
A faithful friend.
It was a gift to you.
It was the greatest gift that could ever have been endowed on you.
It doesn't matter what defects it has.
How imperfect you believe it is.

No one in history has ever been perfect.
No one.
Ever.

You stand among heroines, queens, princesses, saints, actresses,
writers, poets, musicians.
You stand there.
No different to anyone who has ever existed.
No different to anyone who will exist.
Always remember that.

Your body is part of what makes you unique.
It is the shell which protects your very essence.
Your very humanity.
Your soul.
Treat it with the respect that you would give your most precious
possessions.

Keep it healthy.
Treat it with love.
Treat it with care.
Don't despise it.
Don't neglect it.
Don't hurt it.
Pamper it.
Dress it up.
Decorate it.
Soothe it.
Enjoy it.

And that glow of love that you will feel for your body from this
moment onwards will extend to your inner self and how you feel
about that which lies within you.

And the glow will radiate out from you and like a moth to a flame
you will attract others to you.

Because just as you see yourself and rejoice,
You will see everyone through different eyes.
And you will rejoice in their beauty.

And they will rejoice in yours.
Because if you feel beautiful about yourself.
Joyful about yourself.
And celebrate yourself.
So will others.
I promise.

Because you are unique.
Because you are beautiful.
Simple fact.
So my friend, what are you waiting for?

So Lovely

We're conceived as beautiful and born into the world ignorant of any other belief than that. Why can't things just stay the same? Forever....

You're perfect.

Every inch of you.
Every tiny facet.
Every drop of blood.
Every beat of your tiny heart.
Every tiny hair and tiny nail which is growing.
In readiness.

Perfect.

I can feel how perfect you are.
I can feel it as you move slowly around.
An elbow here and a heel there.
Thrusting out of my huge stomach as you stretch and turn.
A stomach which has been so beautiful since it started to carry you.

And I've proudly stroked it and sung to you and told you stories.
Because I love you.

I felt your first movement.
It was as though a butterfly had fluttered gently.
And I marvelled. And I loved.

Deeply.
Honestly.

And I know that you are lovely. And perfect.
I don't want anyone ever to tell you anything different.

In a few weeks you'll enter into this world.
This strange, new, adventurous and magical world.
And you'll start your journey.

I can shield you from anything.
I can protect you from harm.

I'll teach you to look at yourself and smile.
To touch your toes and suck your fingers and delight in twisting
your hair around your hand.

You'll pat your tummy and squeal and rub hands across your face,
feeling the smooth surface.

I'll tell you you're beautiful every day. I'll hold you close and let
the scent of your body permeate my nostrils and you'll laugh when
I pull silly faces.
And we'll rub noses together and gurgle in joy..

And most of all we'll smile and rejoice in each other.
And when you meet other children I'll tell you they're beautiful too.

And you'll want to touch their hands and feel their faces and pull
their hair.
Because they'll be reflections of what you are. Who you are.

And when you look in the mirror you'll see the beauty that shines
from your eyes, and it will make you smile back at yourself in joy.

Then one day you'll leave my protection and venture into the
world. Away from my care.

And others may not tell you that you're beautiful, but you must always tell them that they are.

And others may be harsh and unthinking and cruel.

But you must always be kind and loving and warm.

And then when you look in the mirror you'll see beauty reflected back at you.

And if other children say unkind things, you can run back into my arms and nestle into my body and I'll remind you how beautiful you are.

And in your heart you'll know that anyway. Because I always told you.

For in my eyes you will always be the picture of perfection.

Pretty and lovely and sweet.

My child.

My creation.

My hope.

And when you are too old to fall into my arms and the world is cruel and unkind, you'll remember the reflection in the mirror and venture there again.

And you'll see your eyes and see what's behind them and love the image that is reflected back at you.

And no matter what anyone says to you or makes you feel, always remember that when you were born you were perfect and that hasn't changed.

Only the shell in which you live has changed. Aged, mellowed, grown.

But the beauty is still there.

Deep within. Impossible to lose. Impossible to change.

Embrace it. Feel it. Live it.
Teach your own children the same.
And their children will learn too.

And a small and tiny part of this huge world will change.
For the better.

And always remember.
You're beautiful.
You're lovely.
You're perfect.

Pivot

Our innocence and positive self-image can be shattered by one pivotal moment in time

I know just how you feel.
No really. I do.
I know that in a single moment our lives can change.
Mine did.
My whole concept of who I was and the place I held in this world was altered.

And I never got it back.

Overwritten and then erased. Gone forever.

You see I had this image of myself.
An image that rested at the back of my mind.

It was a nice image. A familiar image. I was comfortable with it.

But then, in a single moment it became distorted, and I didn't know it then, I was too young, but I would never look back and recapture the old familiar me.

It's a shame that I was so young really. It means that I've carried this feeling around with me forever.

And it's influenced how I feel about myself, my body, my relation-ships, my own self-worth.

I guess it must have happened to you too.

That moment. The one that kick started the doubts.

I took almost 35 years to find mine. To identify it and raise it up and relive it.

And in doing that.

In identifying that pivotal moment in time, I came to realise something about myself.

It doesn't change anything. It just helped me.

To understand myself better.

Maybe. If I tell it to you. It might help you.

If you need it. Recognise it. In yourself.

Okay, imagine being eleven.

I had proudly stood by the front gates of my brand new school. My mother had kissed me and given me one last push on my way. I was leaving my old friends behind but was so excited about making new ones. So excited.

I was carefree. Happy. Confident. Ahead, through those gates lay my future. A senior school. Very nice. Very clever girls went there. My mother had always told me I was clever and so I believed her. We always believe what our mothers tell us. They don't lie. They have no reason to. So I was unprepared. But I didn't realise it.

I remember I had tight brown curls and I smiled a lot. I've seen photographs of me when I was little. I looked so happy then. I treasure those.

I clutched my school bag tightly in a hall where hundreds of other girls stood silently waiting for the Head Teacher to greet us at morning assembly.

It all seemed so important. Things do at that age. Without worldly worries. The little things matter. So I listened hard.

Then the girl next to me turned.

I flashed a smile. Maybe she could be my friend. I was desperate to somehow belong in this strange new world. To have a companion to walk the new adventure with me. I was so trusting. So naïve. We all are. At eleven.

I can still see her now. A snapshot in glorious colour. Imprinted on my memory.

Her eyes were green and her hair was the colour of light burnished copper tied in a single flat braid.

Detail.

Does it seem stupid, irrelevant, to remember such detail?

Well let me tell you. It matters. A lot. To me.

Because in that moment, as her mouth opened and she leaned across to my ear to whisper, the balance of my life shifted.

I realise it now. And it hurts. Deep in the pit of my stomach.

I can hear her voice, see the eyes as they flashed. I know now that the look she gave me was cruel.

I've learned what cruelty can be. It was my first taste and it was bitter.

I think the words were almost in slow motion. That's how it seems now. Probably they weren't. But I was only eleven, and I was trusting and eager to hear what she was saying. Perhaps she was going to ask me my name or give me a welcome.

As the words tumbled out, something inside of me died.

It twisted and screamed and tore at my insides.

I can feel it. Even now.

"Ugly parrot nose."

I couldn't speak. My heart had stopped. For a single second I stared at her.

Then I turned away.

I tried to glimpse my nose through the corner of my eye. I couldn't see it.

As we walked slowly in a snake-like formation up the stairs my eyes pricked with tears. And my heart broke.

That night I stood alone in the bathroom and stared at my face. Gone were the pretty eyes and the confidence. I saw what I'd never seen before.

I saw my nose.

It was a hook. A parrot face. Ugly and big, and I was devastated.

My mother had never told me I had an ugly nose. No one ever had.

I shouted at her.

I shouted at my father. They were to blame. Why hadn't anyone warned me? I felt betrayed.

Does that sound dramatic? Betrayed over a nose?

Well it wasn't. I had trusted my parents so implicitly. Trusted that there was nothing anyone could say to me which could take away from the wonderful, innocent and unsullied way I felt about myself and in a split second, in the time it took for that girl to say those three words to me, I'd been proved wrong. And in my eyes they'd been shown up to be flawed. They'd failed me.

So yes, I felt betrayed.

And in that single moment I went from loving myself to hating myself.

My insides screamed every time someone mentioned my nose.

Why couldn't they see the rest of me?

What was so fascinating about a big nose?

I never found out.

For years I suffered at the hands of the taunts and the comparisons to ugly people on television, in the films.

One day I asked a girl I knew, why she'd done it. Why she'd teased me. Taunted me. She said it was because she could. That there had been a vulnerability about me. Even though she had stopped several years earlier, others hadn't.

I knew she was right. About my vulnerability.

And where there's vulnerability there has to be a way of shoring it up. Of throwing up the defences and of changing things. Of protecting myself from further hurt.

And so I made a decision that day.

I made an appointment with a plastic surgeon.

The surgeon said he'd even tipped my top lip upwards to make it prettier.

The parrot nose was gone.

Consigned to the past.

And so I reinvented myself.

I grew out my hair and I bought new clothes.

I had dates. Lots of them.
I got married.
I had children. Beautiful children.

I was different. More confident. I felt pretty again.
I'd changed.
At least I thought I had.

You see fate is a cruel woman.
She lulls us into false securities. Which are fleeting.
And then she beckons us in. Just when we feel safe.
She reminds us of our insecurities and the pivotal moments in our lives.

And so one day she pointed a finger at me.
And lured me towards her, and to a chance meeting, which reminded me that despite changing my appearance I could never actually change me.

A woman who'd taunted me at school arrived at my place of work.

She looked straight past me and noticed a photograph of my two children on my desk.

My beautiful children.

She didn't comment on how I now looked. I was invisible. She only saw what she thought she saw.

"Well thank goodness they didn't get your nose, eh?" she said, and laughed.

And in that instant, I knew. I'd worked out what had triggered the insecurities. The poor body image. The low self-esteem.

Because she reminded me.

I knew that in essence the outside of my face was only a shell.
That in truth I was damaged on the inside.
Okay, the image was different. The nose was gone.
Generally, people complimented me all the time on how I looked.
They still do. Except that one person.

But inside I'm still screaming.
I'm still remembering that pivotal moment. We all have one.
We think we've buried it.
But it will always reach up a hand and drag us in. When we least expect it.

When self-doubt rears its ugly head.
I know that no matter how hard I try.
I always will be. Frightened. Insecure.

The little girl who stood there that morning and died inside.

Booby Prize

If Kate can't persuade you that coveting big boobs is a bad idea then no one will!!

I can't believe you're thinking about wanting big breasts?

You are, aren't you?

Seriously?

Like really, really big breasts?

Oh come on now! Think about it!

Seriously, sit back and think hard before you wish for something like that.
No, don't take it lightly. Because what you're going to end up with sure as hell aren't going to be light.
Oh no, they'll be a pair of heavyweights. Yep.

And pendulous.
Not to mention back breaking.
Oh, and did I mention, neck crunching?
In fact, face it, you'll have great, big, massive bazookas!

And it's no picnic. Let me tell you.
It's not all low cut bikinis and bouncing along a beach with a bunch of hot guys in the sun.

Oh they'll stare at you all right. A lot of men will look. But not at your eyes.

And your girlfriends won't be much help, either. Depending on whether they've got nothing up top or know what reality is really like, they look at you with either sympathy or envy.

We all know a lot of men like big-breasted women.
Seriously, I know it too. I do. Okay?
They stare and they lust.

BUT they don't have to lie down in bed, turn over and then wait two minutes for their breasts to follow.
Or get back ache or shoulder ache from bra straps straining to hold those babies in place.

I guarantee you all. If they did, all the advertising - everywhere - would be for small-breasted women.
I'd take a great pair of small, neat breasts any day.

And sports?
Don't even go there.

Okay here's a scenario to consider.
So you just got the ultimate boob job done.
You're feeling good and very excited. Ready to show them off.

First thing you do - join that gym you've always stared at, right?
Of course you do. You want to impress!
Not just yourself but everyone around you.

Whoa!
Reality check!
So now you've got the big ones you've always wanted.
Breasts you are so proud of you want to show the world the new you.

But sister, anything which entails your body moving past a snail's pace usually means your tits bounce right along with you.

If you're lucky and you don't get brained by all that leaping up and down, your nipples will be so sore when you've finished you'll be praying your breast surgery was all a dream.

It's only perfect on television, folks.

And yes, I know what you're thinking. She's forgotten sports bras. That'll be the answer.

Seriously, you can forget it. If you do manage to get one to stretch across your new cup size, chances are the strain will break the clasp at the back and you'll be showing more of your new cleavage to that hunk of a Trainer than you ever imagined!

And while we're on the subject of getting out there and showing off your new cleavage, let's talk about spas.

After all, it's the ultimate relaxation in a stressful world.

Well it is for most people….

So, you see the ad in the paper.
You're tempted.

It looks so relaxing. All your friends go. They've told you about those treatments.

A glorious facial. A hot oil massage.
Mmm….sounds good.

I'm really sorry to burst the Zen bubble you've just wrapped around yourself, but honestly you'd be better forgetting it.

Surprised?

Okay, it looks like you're going to take some convincing.

Have you ever tried lying flat on your stomach with two melons stuck out in front?
I really can testify to that one.
I tried it. Got all excited about relaxing and having the full body massage and then I lay down.

All I looked like was someone intent on trying out some new yoga position. Awkwardly.

You know that part of the massage table where your face sticks through so you can breathe?

My guess is a man designed the bloody table.

Why don't they make a table with two holes neatly cut where a woman can let her boobs fall in and relax?

I know! It sounds obvious, doesn't it?

Now there's a thought! Maybe I should patent that idea myself.

Ooh and let's talk pregnancy, too.

In case you didn't already know it, there is one sure fire method in this world designed to make a girl's boobs expand more quickly than anything else.

Get pregnant. It's like attaching a helium cylinder. Instant cleavage boost. Sounds pretty exciting, doesn't it?

Something to look forward to, eh?

Well, a pregnant woman is a beautiful act of nature. No doubt about that.

Trouble is, things kind of - get in the way - before the baby comes along.

I used my new, improved cleavage as a shelf to rest my coffee on one time.

Baby kicked and, yes, you guessed it, coffee all over my best friend sitting next to me. Handy, huh?

If you haven't been put off big breasts by now, perhaps this one last thing will clinch it.

Age.

Girls, it's a sad fact of life that when you reach a certain age your body decides it wants to spend its retirement in more southerly climes.

You know. South. Helped by gravity.

And trust me. There are no palm trees where those body parts start heading.

The boobs, and the larger they get the more they do it, head south first.

I like to think of it as a relaxing of the musculature.

Okay, fine, it's sagging.

You've all heard the phrase: 'The bigger they are, the harder the fall'?

Oh you can look just as pert and as held in place as you like when you're fixed in that bra you took a mortgage out for.

But come sundown, when you unhitch it and finally exhale?

It takes a few minutes. But oh, there…

Down they go.

I hate to disillusion you, girls, but it happens to everyone.

So, there it is, plain and boring. The unadorned truth about big boobs.

So. After you've heard all that.

If you're still coveting bigger boobs.

Ask yourself one question.

For God's sake, woman!

WHY?

Nice Things Come
In Small Packages

Felicity gives us a poignant view of the other side of the boob debate

I'm going to tell you a story. It's about me. But it's also not about me. It's about a journey.

There's only one thing I hated about myself. One thing I really, really wanted.

I wanted boobs!!!

All those girls who talk about hating their size double E cup boobs made me as green as grapes. I mean I felt like I got left out when they were handing out the womanly attributes. You know like someone got distracted just when they reached me and forgot those bits up top. If I could have gone back in time I'd shout, "Hey, hold on just a minute. You forgot something. I need those. I need them so I can be a whole woman."

And I'd have forced them to go back and make things right.

Do you think I was being overly sensitive? Come on, when they put all the little girls in the same room and the Health teacher started explaining the facts of life, and she talked about how our bodies would change. I got kind of excited. All of us did. I was supposed to get boobs. It would happen. Everything would be alright. Finally.

Then what happened? Did my boobs get lost or did one of my class-mates get double boobs? I remember waiting patiently, and wait-ing…and waiting.

My friends all got boobs. Mine started to grow. Minutely. Then they stopped. Almost as if they'd been stunted in their growth. Like two fried eggs. Small and flat and barely rising in the middle. Never destined to leave the frying pan. No amount of cooking was going to change that.

I sulked. Then I panicked. Then I sulked again.

My little sister suffered alongside me. Watching for mine to sprout she got more and more anxious when hers didn't either. Then finally, when I was in college, my little sister and I cornered my mum one night about our lack of boobs. Mum just smiled and said we'd prob-ably get boobs with pregnancy. She said she had. I joked and said that maybe it was time I got pregnant then.

Note to those of you thinking "oops, maybe that wasn't a good idea." Yep. You're right. It's not the smartest thing to say to your mother.

It's been hard even to go shopping for clothes. I have this friend who always moaned that her chest was too big to look great in sweaters. Like someone is looking at her boobs all the time. Honestly. I tried telling her she looked great. She didn't believe me. So she dressed to take attention away from them.

Me, I felt like I wasn't sexually attractive on the basis that I have a small chest.

Whatever I put on just hangs. Sometimes you can glimpse my nipples through a top if it's clinging to me in the heat of summer. But mostly they're my invisible friends.

Only six months ago I'd been flicking through the rails in a shop and a woman standing near to me held up a jacket to her girlfriend and laughed.

She said she could only wear it if she wasn't a "real woman" with no breasts.

It's not a terrible comment and maybe I'm being hypersensitive but when you've been a victim to the same comments for so many years, been poked in the chest and told that you're as flat as a pancake, or had your so-called friends call your bras 'eye patches', hearing that sort of comment stings.

I know a lot of these supermodels have no boobs. But when I look at them parading down the catwalk all I see is tall elegant women. No boobs maybe, but they look great anyway. And the reporters and those glossy magazines are all over them. They're considered attractive.

But me, I'm no super model. I'm five foot three inches tall. I'm not skinny. I'm not fat. My rear is larger than I'd like but that problem pales into insignificance when I'd catch sight of myself in the mirror and see this flat-chested "woman" staring back at me and loathing myself.

And it was a loathing. A feeling that no man was ever going to like me, or want me, because an important part of my anatomy, which shouts out that I'm a woman isn't nearly good enough.

But then one evening everything changed.

The furthest thing from my mind that night, were my boobs. Seriously.

For someone who had become self absorbed in the rather boyish look to her upper torso, for a change I found myself distracted by the woman across the Underground carriage from me. Her eyes were red, swollen in fact and she was staring into space.

YOU IS FOR UNIQUE

I remember thinking how haunted she looked. As if her world had come tumbling in suddenly and she had no one to turn to. I remember looking at her face and thinking how pretty she was, that despite the tears, she was attractive and vivacious and didn't deserve to be feeling whatever it was that was causing her such distress.

I also remember feeling this overwhelming urge to go over and hug her and tell her that whatever it was that was making her feel so terrible I'd make better.

Can you imagine? I mean a complete stranger on a train. Whatever was I thinking?

She might be some psycho who would view my unwanted sympathy with disgust, draw some sort of a knife and that would be the end of me. I almost mentally wrote the tragic headline for the morning paper as I got out of my seat and found myself moving across towards her, propelled by....I don't know what.

I can't repeat our entire conversation that evening. Some of it was, in the end, intensely personal. Some of it I'll remember for the rest of my life. Because that evening my life changed. My perception of myself changed.

And it changed because I had to change. Inside.

Her name was Laura. She viewed my sitting next to her warily but when I put a hand on hers and asked her if I could help, the tears poured down her face. Despite the handful of people dotted around our carriage, she talked.

Over the next six months Laura and I became friends. After her double mastectomy, chemotherapy and recuperation her breast cancer was declared gone. They remodelled the tissue and created new nipples for her. We shopped together, both sporting fried egg sized boobs, but both proud. We wore clothes we liked, not what we thought everyone else would like.

She's my best friend.

In some ways, although she says that I was sent as an angel to support her and be with her, I believe she was sent to support me. But more, she showed me what really matters in life. She showed me because I had to show her. That my body was perfect as it was.

That the fact that I had tiny boobs meant nothing.

I was, and am, still a woman.

Beautiful, sensual, confident in my appearance and sexy.

And I know that because I had to persuade Laura, that cold night on that Underground train, that her biggest fear, of no longer being a woman, was unfounded.

Look at me! I had tiny boobs, so small you needed a microscope to see them, and I felt all woman.

Laura believed me. I found myself believing me.

I realised that night that our bodies are what we have.

Sure we can enhance them, make them bigger or better or smaller. But in the end the thing that makes us women can't be found in a cup size.

My grandmother always used to say, *"Nice things come in small packages."*

I couldn't have said it better.

Bountifully Bootylicious

Welcome to the world of big, bold and beautifully proud

Listen to me girlfriend. I'm sorry but I can't swim.
I tried, but I mean I just can't.
I take one look at my ass in that swimsuit and pull the damn thing off.
Ain't goin' there.

You wanna know what I think I look like? Really?

A whale.
A huge, black whale floating around in the water is what I know I look like.

Even that leopard skin swimsuit I tried on ain't gonna disguise no whale.

Anyhow, the last time I jumped into a pool they spent the next day clearing the water from the terraces two storeys above.

Okay, I know, I'm kiddin' you honey, but you get my drift.

And as for a gym!

Do you know how many mirrors one room can have?

I ain't paying to see a hundred damn reflections of my sorry ass squeezed into tight lycra.

I know what I look like, girl.
Don't need no Personal Trainer tellin' me to shake it and to lose it.

I don't wanna lose it.
I like it just the way it is.

And as for that crazy runnin' machine.

Shit! Baby if you're lucky your tits stay intact and don't go into orbit
one at a time while you try and stay upright.

Trust me! It ain't a pretty sight.
I'm sorry, but exercise and me just ain't made for each other.
You understand what I'm sayin'?

Now threads. That's a whole different story, girl.

Real threads. Okay, now you're gonna see somethin'.

Fashion icons eat your damn hearts out!
I love my clothes, struttin' my stuff and lookin' good.
Forget getting naked or wearing some damn swimming costume so
tight it screams at you when you tug it down.

And you wanna really know somethin'?
I don't feel bad about myself. You might wanna think I do, but I sure
as hell don't.

Baby, I loves my body.

Overweight. Obese. Fat. Call it what you wanna. I've been called it
all and worse.

I'm just a big girl. Always have been. Always will be.

Loads to grab a hold of. Loads to love. My momma always told me
I was, "so bootiful" men would fall at my feet

Well it's true. I had a man fall at my feet once.

Between us, I think he was kinda drunk when he fell over.

But I got me a good man. He's a looker and he's all mine.

And I get plenty of exercise all of my own.
Don't need me no gym.
Get my drift, honey?

Being big ain't all that bad.

See, I got boobs some chicks would die for.

I got curves where curves ain't supposed to be.

I'm all woman that's for sure.

Why would I want to be some scrawny little thing?

I look at some of these girls and man, they're gonna break as soon
as you look at them.

A man gets his arms around me and he ain't gonna break nothin'.
And he's got plenty to hang onto.

I got ebony skin so smooth it don't need no creams to keep it
like that.

And I just love my nails. I got the stars and stripes all over them and
they're as long as I ever wanted them to be.

My momma always told me that I was growing up to be a big girl.
She was kinda big herself.

Thinkin' about it, my grammie was a big momma too. I guess
I kinda come from a long line of big women.

And they were so happy. They dressed themselves up for Sunday Service with them big hats and their fancy shoes. My momma used to tell me that it was the only day she ever dressed up. They strutted their stuff and they were proud of it and I used to sit on my momma's lap and, man, life was real good.

I'm proud.

I don't wanna be skinny. I just don't wanna be.

I want to be big and bootiful like my momma and my grammie and I ain't gonna change cause some magazine tells me that some skinny white girl is what I gotta look like.

How d'ya think I'd look as some skinny blonde haired girl?

Yeah. You sure are right. I'd look so stupid my momma would turn in her grave, God bless her.

And sure, there's a lot of black skinny girls out there making it large in the movies and strutting their skinny asses down the catwalk.

And sure they're as bootiful as us big girls, but I don't wanna be like them.

I wanna be like me. I wouldn't know how to be if I was all skin and bones. No.

All these advertising films on the television, they never show us big women.

Why not? I mean from what I can see out there on the street there sure are more of us than there are of them skinny young things.

It ain't democratic. We ain't represented.

One of my girlfriends is a big white girl with attitude. She struts her stuff and wears her threads and has a good time.

She don't wanna be skinny either.

I know big folk and I know skinny folk and some are good and some are bad.

Some are happy and some sure as shit ain't.

Size don't make your world. What you are is what makes your world. I guess the world just gotta come around to accepting we all ain't the same.

Tryin' to make us feel bad about what we are, when we don't feel bad.

Some of us are big and some of us are small.

Live with it.

Distortion

Twenty-five year old Bethany had let others destroy her life.
Now she is fighting back.

I'm bulimic.
There, I said it. Bulimic.

Better to get it right out in the open. Throw it in your face so you can do the "sharp intake of breath and shuffle with embarrassment in your seat" bit and get it over and done with.

And then perhaps you'll listen.

Because people don't admit to being bulimic.

Face it, it's not the coolest thing to say to people.

Hey how are you?

Well, actually I'm bulimic. In a minute, when we leave this restaurant, I'm going to go home and chuck my guts up, stand up, wipe my chin and look in the mirror and still feel fat.

Oh.

Yep. A real party pooper. A real show stopper and conversation killer.

Bulimia!!!

But I'm standing here tonight because I want to tell you how it started.

How I used to be.

And how I feel about myself right now.

So you'll understand.

And maybe things can change.

For someone else.

Before it's too late.

Because maybe you'll know someone like me.

Or maybe you are someone like me.

And maybe this will help.

I'm praying it will.

Don't be embarrassed. I'm not.

I'm afraid. And I'm really pissed off and angry. At me.

See. When I was young I was okay really. Not particularly skinny, but okay as things go.

Never thought about what I looked like. I mean, when you're in your pre-teens, things don't matter so much, do they?

And then I hit puberty. And there it was. The first five pounds. Not much.
It didn't matter.

I didn't care what people thought.
To hell with them.
If they didn't like me, tough luck.

But then the next three pounds appeared.

And suddenly it mattered. It mattered a lot.

I still don't know why.
Something kind of clicked. Like a light switch inside me.

The girls in my year at school got interested in clothes and fashion and what people looked like in magazines. They wanted to be like them.

And most of them dressed so they were.

They looked at me.
And I wanted to be the same. But I couldn't. Because I wasn't skinny like them.

I had what my mother called "puppy fat".

But wrapping it up in some sentimental label didn't make it go away.

I desperately wanted this sweater that I'd seen all the other girls wearing.

Because by wearing it, maybe I'd be like them. Finally fit the image everyone wanted for me.

But when my mum bought it for me. Saved and scrimped and bought it for me. And I put it on. I didn't look any different.

I still looked fat.

And then the teasing started. The cruel words and the comments.

I started to look at myself and feel their hate and hated myself too.

I started to eat crazy things. Combining foods that you'd never combine. They'd make me feel ill to look at, but eating them made me feel better.
Took away the pain of the torment and the cruelty. Comforted me.

I used to eat in secret. So no one would know what I was doing.
I bet you're thinking, *why didn't she turn to her parents?*
Why didn't someone help her?

See, I didn't have it easy at home. Things were bad. Nobody had any time for me. So I ate more.

And the problem got worse.

And I know now that if I'd gone and got some help or turned to someone maybe I wouldn't have done what I did next. But there wasn't anybody. At least not anybody I thought wouldn't laugh at me.

Wouldn't tell me to get a grip and look around me at the rest of the world and count myself lucky.

I couldn't risk that. So I kept it to myself.
Then one day I decided that if I made myself sick, it wouldn't matter what I ate.
It wasn't something I planned. It just happened.
I don't know why I thought that. I mean what a stupid thing to think. But I did.
And when I made myself sick I felt better.
I felt in control. I had something over those bullies.
Despite what they were doing to me, I had a secret control of my body.

It felt like the only control I'd ever had in my life. Ever.

I lost weight. A lot of weight. But when I looked in the mirror, nothing had changed.
I was fat. My hips were too big.

So I kept being sick. Just a little bit.

When I made myself sick, I felt in control.
Control of my weight. Control of my life.

But I screwed it all up.
I'm still young, but I'm damaged beyond anything I ever imagined.

Sure I got control of my life. I controlled how fast I destroyed my body.
My teeth are a mess.
My insides look like somebody broke in and shot the place up with a semi-automatic.
And I've damaged my heart.
How stupid is that?
Why would anyone knowingly damage their own heart?

Call me an idiot.

Just say it.
I know I do.

But I'm still standing here. So maybe I'm not that dumb.
Anymore.

My friends, they don't call me stupid. They try to help me.
I finally found people I can talk to. People I wish had been there years ago.

And it's because of them that I'm alive.
I'm trying not to give in.

So often.

I've only been sick twice each week for the last month.
That might not sound much better. But it's huge.

I'm proud again. I can smile.

And I want all of you to know something.

I hate that the bullies won.
I hate that I let them.
I hate that they made me feel so bad I did this to myself.

I want people to stop and think.
You don't need a gun or a knife to kill someone.
They tried to sign my death sentence. With words.

But I'm fighting back.

Yes, I'm bulimic.
Yes, my body is damaged.
But they're not in control anymore.

I'm going to stand here right now.
I'm going to look you in the eye. And I'm going to say:

Next week, I'll only be sick once.

Beauty Secret

Tamsin's feelings about herself are special

I am beautiful.

I have shining long brown hair, which glistens when the sun catches it.
I have full lips which part to reveal straight white teeth.
Blue, blue eyes.
My skin is soft and clear.
My fingers are long and slender and my nails are a pretty pink.

I'm told my smile lights up a room.
I blush when people tell me that.
It's difficult to see my smile when I look in the mirror.
I'm sure it looks forced when I'm trying to smile at myself.

I can create exciting stories and beautiful poems and songs.

I write lovely letters and I have so many friends it's hard to keep up.
I love people.
I can't dance. But lots of people can't dance.
My mother says it doesn't matter that I can't dance. She never could either.

I can paint. Colourful pictures of places I've never been to.

Palaces and gardens I've seen on the television.

I love colour and pattern and depth.

I love the clothes I wear. I love shopping for pretty tops. Pretty skirts. I love shoes. But they are more difficult to find.

And mostly I'm happy. So very happy.

I'm so lucky.

I live in a lovely house.

I have my own room.

I have my own computer.

I have a wonderful family.

I'm loved.

I have a pet dog called Sissy who makes me laugh, and cuddles up to me at night for warmth. And kisses me when she thinks I'm upset, and licks away my tears if she sees them fall.

I have an older sister who tells me I'm beautiful every day of the week. Who sits and talks to me. Tells me about life at her school. Teaches me things only sisters can teach you. And paints my nails for me, and giggles with me when she's doing my hair with her new hair straightener.
And wraps her arms around me when I'm sad.
And promises to always be there for me.

I go to a swimming pool with her every week.
And when I'm in the water I feel so happy.
So elated.
So free.

I escape my body.
Just for a while.

Because as lovely as my body is.
As beautiful as I am.
As happy as I am.
As fortunate as I am.
As loved as I am.

I can't move.

You see, I was born with severe cerebral palsy.
I'll be in a wheelchair for the rest of my life. But I feel fortunate.
There are so many people worse off than me. I am blessed.
You see, I know I'm beautiful.
And it doesn't matter that I can't prance up and down some catwalk
with long legs and a curvy figure.
It doesn't matter that I'm not a film star or a pop star and never
will be.
Because that's all an illusion.
And I'm not.

I'm real.

And beautiful things are always in my mind.
And so they're in my eyes.
I see the look on my sister's face when she brushes my hair.
The love and joy she has when she's around me.

And I see it on the faces of my friends when they come over to chat.
And I can tell in the words that people write to me when they read
my poetry on the Internet.
Poetry that has taken me days to write, because it's so difficult to
control my fingers on the keyboard, and it's time consuming, and
sometimes frustrating.

And I see the joy in the faces of people when they see my paintings.
Paintings I've done using a brush that I often hold in my mouth,
because it doesn't shake so much.

And when my sister puts makeup on my face and holds the mirror so that I can see, I usually have to stop myself from crying.
Because I do look beautiful.

And even though my words are slurred sometimes, I can laugh and tell jokes and most important of all I can tell everyone how much I love them.
And that is so important to me.

It's probably the most important thing about feeling beautiful.
To tell people how wonderful they are and share that feeling with them.
So they feel beautiful too.

Sometimes people will pass me on the street.
And their eyes turn away in embarrassment.
They never see mine.
And I know then that they've missed it.
My beauty.

And they haven't given me a chance to tell them how beautiful they are.
That makes me sad.
That they missed out.

But I'm sad for them. Not me.
Because I'll always hold the secret deep inside of how lovely I feel.

What I feel about myself is all mine.

Being lovely is real.
It's not an illusion.
I know.
Because I am.
So lovely.

Unbeliever

Francesca is beautiful. Why is it that she can't love herself?

Do you know how hard it is to believe someone loves you?
When you don't love yourself.
Have you ever hated what you see in the mirror so much that when
your husband or lover touches you gently on the shoulder, you recoil
in panic in total incomprehension as to why they would?

How could he find me attractive?
When I'm not.
How could he have chosen me in the first place?
When there are hundreds and thousands of women more beautiful
than me.

Out there.
A world of beauty. And yet he chose someone who isn't.

How could he want to make love to me, when my body isn't an
image of perfection?
Far from it.

How can I feel sexy?
When I know I don't look sexy?
I've always known that to be attractive means to have slender legs
that rise so high it's impossible to tell where they end.

To have a flat lean stomach, slim hips and a waist he can put his
hands around and not have to use half of his arms as well.

To have breasts which don't droop and which are just big enough and not too small, and not too large.

To have perfect features and long hair, which shines as the sun catches it in the morning.

I know because I've seen it.

Out there on the television.

In the magazines.

I've seen it.

To be attractive means perfection.
To be attractive means not to be me.

I've spent my life in doubt and denial.
Doubt that anyone could find me remotely attractive in the first place.

Denial that when they said they did, they were telling the truth.

I wondered if he just wanted a good wife more than an attractive partner. I could be that. I could be a good wife, a good mother, a good friend.
It felt warm to think I didn't need to be anything special.

I could just be....imperfect.

I couldn't be a pin up girl or a great example of those perfect actresses you see all the time on the television and on the movies.

The ones who always get the good-looking men.
The fantastically kind men.
The heartbreakingly adorable men.
The heroes.

Have you ever seen a hero go for the plain girl, the overweight girl, the skinny girl, the ugly girl?
Doesn't happen.

If it doesn't happen in the movies why would it happen in real life?

And yet my husband is good looking, fantastically kind and adorable. So how did that happen?

And then there are my friends. What do they see in me? What on earth is there about me that they'd possibly like?

They must be lying. Yes that's it. They're feeding me lies.

And yet I don't know why they would lie. So I make up reasons. It doesn't matter if they're true. Or real.

But seriously, what do my friends see in me? What on earth is beautiful about me?
I don't understand it. I'll never understand it.

I love them with all my heart. I tell them that.
But when they tell me the same, I smile an embarrassed smile and file the comment away somewhere so that I don't have to think about it again.

I try to imagine it's just false flattery.
Because it must be.
Because I'm not lovable.

You know I've actually told myself that if I can look at my friends, none of whom is perfect, and love them and find them stunningly beautiful, then why can't I accept that they see the same in me?
I look into their eyes and see their inner beauty.
The inner beauty that shines and makes them beautiful on the outside.
I can see it.

I accept that they think they see it in me. But they're wrong.
To believe that in some way I am beautiful means I have something
to live up to.

I can't go there.
It's too difficult.
I'll never live up to those images in the magazines or those actresses
in the films.
I simply can't, and the pressure is too much.
So it's easier to not be beautiful in so many ways.
It's easier to slide into the underworld where the beautiful don't
exist.
Where it's safe.

And so that's where I stay.

I've come to a conclusion.
I can't be beautiful.

Can I?

Net Worth

Kelly inhabits cyberspace at night. Join her for
a walk through the world of the Internet.

When I was Foxxy, the rather buxom sex goddess from the Bronx,
times were good.

Strange that the mere name conjured up an image in men's and
women's minds of some leggy chocolate skinned femme fatale.

I have to admit it conjured up the same image in mine.

I played into it though. I mean Foxxy says as Foxxy does. I had so
much fun. And it was all so safe. Intense but safe.

Of course there was the time that Harold, the wise middle-aged
gentleman from London had the time of his life, and mine, playing
on the forums in complete safety and with life experience to offer in
his travels.

The things men will tell you when they think you're another man.
Oh boy!

My current incarnation is Rachel.

She's a nice safe housewife from London.

She spends her time discussing….well, I guess, discussing all the
things nice housewives from London discuss…life, the world and
everything.

Mostly though we discuss our bodies, their shape, size, proportions and the men in our lives.

It's very enlightening.

At least it would be, if I had a man.

But when I do get a man I'll know a lot more then than I ever knew before.

But, saying that, I've learnt a lot and made friends.

That's the amazing thing. I've made a whole ton of friends over the last five years.
I haven't met any of them in person. And I've discovered a lot about myself.

I've discovered that I can be anything I want to be.
On the Internet you can quite literally manufacture a person, live their life and almost come to believe it yourself.

That's if you've got a screw loose and a few marbles flying around.
Keep grounded and it's all good.
It's a fantastic experience.
It's safe and it's enlightening and it's life altering.

But is it real?
I can be fat, thin, black, white, speak English, speak French, speak Spanish, be male or female, gay or straight or both, young or old when I'm on the Internet.

I can invent a whole life story, which reflects what I want to be, not what I am.
Does that make me feel any worse about myself when I struggle into work the next day?

Does the fact that I can experiment in the safety of my own living space with who I am or want to be, ruin my life?

I can weave a character out of thin air. I can create a life history for the character, sit back and smile and launch my creation on an unsuspecting world.

And they swallow it.
Hook, line and sinker.
I am Dave, or Rachel or Harold or Foxxy or Christie or any other name I invent.

To go on some forums it's safer to pretend to be male.
Less hassle, less unwanted attention.
Safety.
Where else in this world can you do that?
At a club you can't cruise in pretending to be something you're not.
The illusion wouldn't hold.
Discovery, the instant penalty.

But on the Internet anonymity rules.

A woman has red hair, a fabulous smile, is slim and vivacious. Her avatar shows it. She sounds like it.

Is she real?

Well no actually, she's my mate Shirl from work who spends a vast proportion of her time perpetuating the myth online that she's exactly that, when in fact she's slightly chubbier than she'd like to be, dark haired, small and a grouch most of the time.

But people buy into it. So does she.

Shirl spends the evening feeling good about herself and crap the next day because she can't live up to the image.

I look down at what I am some mornings and sigh.
My body's not perfect. I'm not a model. I don't have a partner. I'm not particularly into fashion and besides online people don't see your clothes.

Heck, I could be naked for all anyone knows!

But I am loved. I am admired. I'm cherished and I have so many friends I've lost count.

And they've never even seen me.

If they did, I wonder how many of them would be so disappointed that the illusion was shattered they would back away?

I doubt I'll ever know.

Rachel is about to go AWOL a while.

I'm sure her London housewife friends will understand that a trip to Florida is a necessary break from the Internet. You see, Clarissa just said hello to a group of film buffs on a forum and the welcome was so good she thinks she might stay a while...

Reality TV

Marlene explains how hard it is when the world thinks you're perfect

Oh crap…I'm going to bet the tabloids have my face plastered all over the front pages.

You've just got to look at the news alerts this morning on the TV. Yep. I'm dead meat.

Just look at them. Slavering to get a look at my "oh-so-not-honed" body and pasty face. Lenses pointing at my windows, then swinging around to my front door. They think I'm going to grab that milk off the step any second. Well they're wrong!

I'm sure as hell not giving them the satisfaction.

I can see the headlines anyway. *"Actress Lets Herself go in Wake of Angry Split."*

And there it will be. A great big arrow pointing directly at my puffed out ass when I bend over to grab that bottle off the step.

No airbrushing there, sweetheart.

And of course, to add insult to my injury, I'm bra-less as well. God knows what they'd make of that.

How about *"Heading South. Actress in Urgent Need of Help."*

And let's not even talk about my face.

Of course if I wait until the makeup is on and I've heaved those jeans neatly into place…megaton zip in position, they'll be writing the headlines for tomorrow.

"Hiding from the World. A Hermit is Born."

Life's tough.
I wish my agent hadn't happily phoned around every tabloid in town and told them I was splitting up from Tony yesterday.

"My sweet, any way of telling your adoring public that the asshole in your life has departed is good enough for me. The press will love it."

I protested. Of course. Just to be left on my own for a few days at first.

Nope. Fat chance.

"Your fans have a right to know."

No one has a right to know.

No one has a right to a piece of my life, seemingly least of all me.

Oh God. If only I hadn't gone for that huge Italian meal with Carla last night.
I should have waited to make the split from Tony.
Waited until my Trainer had said that my body was toned enough for display in the tabloids.

Waited until my face had stopped exploding into great mountain-like protrusions after a full season's TV work caked in cement-like foundation every day.

One of them seemed to be erupting like Vesuvius yesterday. Its sister volcano was well on the way to an eruption today some time. Watch this space.

Perfection? Me? Not now. I don't think I ever was.

I'm just human. I'm just a woman.

And now I'm a woman in pain.
Back in the public eye, just when I want to crawl under some palm tree and hide, soakin' up the sun and trying to get over stuff. Personal stuff.

God forbid I'd venture onto a beach right now. What am I thinking?

A bikini? Nope. It's not going to happen. If the backside doesn't get filmed, or the boobs get the attention then the kangaroo pouch fondly known as my stomach will.

Stuck in my house.

That's what's going to happen.

Under siege. Internet shopping and visits from sympathetic and curious friends.

Glamorous? I don't think so.

I kind of know why the magazines do it. I kind of understand why people look at those damn photographs and see the real bodies and the real men and women with their guards down.

It must make them feel good. Makes them think we're no more special than they are.

No more perfect than the average woman in the street.

Trouble is, I guess they don't understand the hurt.

Well, I've got news for them.

Truth is, we aren't any more special or more perfect than anyone.

And if people would only understand that, they wouldn't bother looking at those photos or hoping to get a look at us with all our imperfections and compare us to our alter egos on the screen.

Yes, of course we like to look pretty. Yes, that fake tan cost me a ton of money.

What the public wants, the public gets. But reality doesn't exist for any of them.

I'm no different to anyone in the street but no one is going to see that. Ever.

They don't realise what's real. They all want illusions. Fantasies.

They don't see that underneath it all. I'm just me. I've got insecurities. I've got an ass that I don't want, and a stomach that doesn't understand the words "tuck yourself in child".

Tell you what though. My boobs are all mine, sweetheart. They might be migrating but they're doing it all on their own, without any help from anyone or anything.

Listen, I'm heading for 50. I've done the pretty young thing gig.
What am I supposed to do?
Get into some time bubble?
That's just so not real. I've had three kids.

I've got the stomach and the boobs to prove it.

Oh, I've had enough of all this.
And I've had enough of those vultures outside.

To hell with all this crap. I need a coffee.

And I need the milk from that step.

Wish me luck.

Her Suit

Justine decides to speak out.
Razors, shavers, wax and lasers
at the ready! To war ladies!

When I was at school there was a girl who had legs so covered in thick dark hair that people referred to them as "bog brushes".

Nice huh?

Of course they were the teasers and the unthinking bullies who had nothing better to do with their lunchtimes than follow around any poor sod that had anything different about them and taunt them.

She ignored them. She was of Mediterranean parentage, proud of it and had thick curly dark hair and a mellow tanned skin. Her upper lip was graced with a light covering of dark hair as well.

I thought she was beautiful.

I also thought she was the proudest person I'd ever met.

We were friends.

We went swimming together.

We did dancing together.

I didn't notice her hairy legs. She didn't notice my non-hairy legs. I didn't notice her hairy lip. She didn't notice my non-hairy lip. Life was cool.

We were ten years of age and long summers under huge billowing trees talking about the future and the excitement of our plans were all that we were interested in. Our bodies were only then starting to develop. We weren't interested in anything other than having fun.

Maybe deep inside she ached at the taunts, but she never showed it and she never talked about it. She also never shaved her legs or her lip. She probably never shaved anywhere else. But then I didn't ask her about that.

As the years went on I lost contact with my friend. Her life took one path and mine meandered along onto the track I was creating for myself.

But I'll never forget her.

Hitting my twenties was fun. Nothing earth shatteringly interesting to report, apart from a couple of short but annoying hairs snaking their way down from my chin.

A quick trip to the nice lady in the Electrolysis Department at my local Department store and I thought I'd get rid of the pesky buggers. Some women swear by electrolysis. Me? Well, it was painful and it left me with red dots all over my chin. I came out feeling far from attractive but hopeful. Maybe this would be one of my last visits. They say hope springs eternal....

But they were stubborn. So stubborn.

I think a nuclear explosion six inches from my face wouldn't have shifted them.

They just kept coming back....and multiplying.

Figuring that the nuclear explosion was perhaps a beauty step too far and having shelled out far too much of my hard earned money on two measly hairs, which were now breeding like a pair of field mice, I turned to other methods.

Waxing. Ooh painful. My poor chin didn't like that. It screamed and burned and went bright red and the hairs stayed put.

Hair removal cream. You know the stuff that you have to plaster on and then attempt not to move while you're waiting for it to work? Well I tried that for a few years. Limited success, less painful than the other methods but still the march of the facial hairs progressed. And they spread. I now had hairs on my cheeks and hairs on top of my lip.

I remembered my friend.

I looked at the rest of my body. I had hair in the right places. Not too much, not too little. Why was my face so intent on pushing me over the edge?

I started to wonder if it mattered. Hair on face. Not a huge problem in the general scheme of life, the Universe and everything.

But you see it mattered to me. I didn't like the feel of them or the look of them.

I didn't really care what anyone else thought.

Or did I?

And then one day I found out why I was going for a world record in facial hair.

Stand back while I shout this out.

P.C.O.S

What the hell is that all about? Calling something a name as stupid as that?

It sounds like the title of some job in some faceless building where workers share desks and hook into their phones each morning, so that they can communicate with the rest of the world all day and ignore each other.

"Hey go see the PCOS, he's waiting for you."

Sheesh.

About one in ten women of childbearing age has PCOS. It can occur in girls as young as 11 years old.

That's ten percent of the childbearing female population of the world! That's huge!

So give it a name that shows its rightful role in female society. Give it a name that we can remember – don't abbreviate it down to four letters.

We know it's long and complicated.

Polycystic Ovary Syndrome.

But it could be called something a bit easier to remember. A bit more female.

How about Polly. Now that would be great wouldn't it?

Have you got Polly?

Okay on second thoughts, perhaps not.

Back to the saga of the facial hairs.

I was thrilled. A diagnosis. YES! Treatment. YES! A cure. NO!

"WHAT?" I yelled in a slightly hysterical voice at the doctor who stepped back nervously.

"What do you mean you can't do anything about what's there already?"

Trying to back out fast, he told me that there was only a treatment for inhibiting future facial hair growth, not what was there already. He suggested electrolysis.

I threw something at the door as he left and went back to the cream.

And then one day my doctor casually mentioned an experimental study at a Plastic Surgery unit nearby and would I be interested in trying to see if they could laser away the hairs. I nearly hugged her.

I was so excited. Slightly daunted because I had to let the hair grow uninhibited for a few weeks, so that there was plenty for them to work on, but excited nevertheless.

I hadn't seen how much hair I had in a long time. I'd always hit it before it got so bad.

It looked like a man's overnight stubble only longer.
For the couple of weeks before the treatment I would put a hand across my chin if I went anywhere and pull scarves up around my mouth and cheeks. I felt embarrassed.

The laser treatment was, shall we say, interesting. The smell of your own burning flesh is not something to be recommended to the faint of heart. But I persevered.

They persevered.

It didn't work. Apparently my hair had too much red in it. Laser didn't work well on red hair. He told me if I'd been dark haired it would have been fine. Fat consolation.

I asked him what I should do next. I was 35.

"Shave."

I heard the word. Let it filter into my brain and then opened my mouth wide.

"Shave?"

He said that he had to tell a lot of women that. There were no alternatives that would be permanent. Shaving was the last resort. He suggested I hit the local Department Store and buy myself one of *"those men's shavers"*.

Do you know what it feels like to be told you're going to have to shave every day?

Do you know what it feels like to feel unfeminine and suddenly no longer the woman you thought you were?

Well I do. And from what he had said, so did dozens of women before me. And those were just the ones who'd ventured into the clinic there!

All these women. All silent. All coping. All miserably taking in what he'd said. Not sharing with anyone, because they were probably too embarrassed.

Like I was.

I came out of there in a daze. I went home.

Then I cried.

Self pity really. Stupid. I think I let out a few decades of frustration into the tissue box, sniffed and then told myself off.

Then I picked myself up and went shopping.

For a shaver.

Life's not all about what you've got or what it deals you. It's about what you do with what you've got and how you cope with what it deals you.

So I'd have to shave. Big deal.

It's quite funny really.

Every morning elbowing my husband out of the way, so that I can stand next to him in front of the long mirror and shave. It took him time to get used to a shaving partner. He had no choice really.

I might have hairs on my face. I might have to shave.

But I'm still a woman. Still feminine in every other way.

At first, nobody else except my husband, my doctor and my best friend knew.

Then I started telling the odd person. If I shared a hotel room with another female friend I'd warn her about my need to shave.

And when women bemoaned the lightly coloured hairs on their upper lip to me, I would joke that they hadn't got a clue what it was like to be really hairy.

And then they wanted to know what I meant. So I would tell them.

And I found that women understood. Were supportive and interested in what had caused the problem in the first place. Were sympathetic to what I had to put up with.

Some had no idea that the problem existed. They thought it was just a tendency to hairiness in some women.

Others confessed that they too shaved, or had laser treatment or weekly electrolysis sessions.

And I realised that by being open with other women, they were open back to me.

Yes, some were surprised at my forthright confession. Others were just relieved to find a fellow sufferer.

Now you know my secret.

It's seriously about time that women were no longer embarrassed to tell one another they shave, if they do. Or wax, or have treatment in any shape or form.

No longer feel ashamed that they have to tackle a condition not of their own choosing.

No longer made to feel less than feminine.

Why doesn't someone make a nice shaver for a woman? For her face?

They make shavers for every other part of a woman. If someone's seen one, let me know!

Let's face it; ten percent of a child-bearing female population and above are possible purchasers. That's a large market.

It may come as a surprise but smooth skin and hairless faces do not come as a part of the female package in all cases.

Sometimes I hear male stand up comics joking about kissing their old aunts and getting prickled by those little hairs on their chin.

Those comments do sting and I feel a wave of sympathy go out to the old aunts in question being the butt of the joke.

I can't help thinking that a woman comic wouldn't do that.

She'd probably joke about shaving next to her husband every morning!

Upset Tummy

Flabby stomachs are a woman's biggest curse. Or are they?

Oh please! I know you think you've got problems!!!

But seriously, you don't know what a big stomach is!

If you had mine then you'd have something to complain about. What you call big is only a swelling.

You've got a tiny mound compared to my mountain.

I know you don't believe me so let me tell you about what it's really like to have a big stomach and you can decide for yourself.

What it's like to have a proper stomach with a kick ass attitude.

In fact a stomach with a life of its own.

For a start off, if there was a Stomach Abuse Helpline they'd have locked me up a long time ago.
No really. I mean it.

It's been through hell and back.
And all I do is criticise it.

Mental cruelty and physical abuse would be on the charge sheet for sure.

I'm going to whisper this so it doesn't hear but don't tell it, despite everything, I actually feel quite sorry for my stomach.

I mean, I've always expected it to do anything I ask it to do and not complain. So I guess I should have expected some sort of revenge.

How would you like to be cut open then sealed up again?
Expand to accommodate a 10lb baby?
Yes, you heard me right. 10lbs!
It didn't stand a chance.
It really didn't.
Oh, I tried to disguise it for a while.

Hurt its feelings, I guess.
I've shoved it into jeans two sizes too small.

Laid on the floor of my bedroom shoving mounds of flesh ever down. Heaved that zip up with a coat hanger and completely ignored my stomach's protest when it rippled up over the top with a sigh, gasping for air.

Wouldn't you call that physical abuse?
I think the courts would.

I don't understand how some women's stomachs expand to enormous proportions and some women's stay flat.

Did I miss the class on "Achieving a Happy Stomach"?
So some women are all nice and polite to their stomachs and so they stay firm and flat?
Is that how it works?

I never thought I was that cruel.
Not really.

Seriously, my stomach was okay when I was a child.
Well. What I mean to say is that it looked okay.
I mean it expanded when it needed to and stayed fairly flat the rest of the time.
I didn't pay it much attention.

Perhaps it was ignored too much. Perhaps I should have complimented it.
Yes, perhaps that's it. Thrown compliments its way and then it would
have rewarded me with a nice pair of flat abs.

Hey, I'm not asking for perfection here.

Just one tiny victory at the Battle of the Bulge.

But no. Not my stomach.
It rebelled like a grumpy teenager.
It sulked.
I rebuked it.
It ignored me.
It thrust itself way out there and swaggered arrogantly.
How dare it!
I tried everything. I really did.
It became my world. My one and only fixation.

I'd look around and everyone was staring at my stomach and not
at me.

Paranoia set in hard.

Then I got pregnant. Yippee!

For two reasons.

First, a lovely baby was on the way.

Second, my stomach finally had a reason for being big.
Secretly, I think my stomach loved that pregnancy, Tent-like dresses
and freedom from tight jeans at last.

But give a stomach an inch and it'll take a yard. Mine did.

After my daughter was born it got all stubborn again.
Stubborn and mad.
At me.

I tried everything. Sit-ups. Crunches. Visits to the gym.
Nothing worked. Heck, even the stuff that used to work – well sort
of - didn't have the same effect!

"Give me hell, will you?" my stomach thought. *"Here's right back
at you"*.

Serves me right, I suppose.

There's only so much you can expect from a poor, abused stomach.

It's too late now.

She's big and she's flabby, and she's here for the long haul.

More than enough inches to pinch for you, me and a few friends.

Can't exchange her, and it's way too late for a refund.
So I guess I've got to live with her.
Maybe love her just a little bit too.
She's been through a heck of a lot, after all.
My poor, misused, upset tummy.

Wasted

Lucy's image of perfection was unattainable and was killing her and her college counsellor knew it.

This is their story.

It seems like only yesterday when she started coming into my office. I remember the sun was shining the first day she knocked tentatively on the door.

Her hair was neat.
Her legs were crossed.
She had slender ankles and perfectly clean trainers.
Her clothes hung loosely from bony shoulders.
She was beautiful.
She looked no older than my own pre-teen daughter. She admitted she was close to graduation.

We talked for hours.
Sometimes she would cry.
Sometimes I wished my job would allow me to.
Sometimes she would laugh.
I never saw the joke.

She had a sense of peace. A sense of inevitability.
That she held her own destiny in her hands, embraced it and let it go.
Despite her looks she had wisdom older than her years.
And yet she couldn't change.

We reasoned.
We argued.
I sometimes felt so angry that shouting would have been an easy escape route.
But I wanted her to keep coming back.
Back to the only person in her life that she talked to.

I felt like her only hope.
I sometimes felt so desperate that I wanted to hug her to me and tell her that if she would just listen, listen to my voice of reason, everything would be alright.

Everything would go away. She could be "normal".

She smiled when she arrived.
She smiled when she left.

In between, her moods ranged from anger to frustration.
From sheer exhaustion to a vitality I'd love to see in all my students.
She became my focus.

My God, she had such an ethereal quality about her.

A transparency that transcended this world. I can see her now.
She was beautiful.
And yet she couldn't see it.

I stood her in front of the mirror and showed her.
She shook her head and laughed, pushing her chin upwards and stroking it.

"At least you don't have a double chin."

Her whisper was almost inaudible as she turned large expressive eyes in my direction. They were moist with tears ready to fall.

"You don't either." I said, it almost pleadingly.

Our conversations had a depth I didn't find in many of my students.
She knew about the world. Embraced it. Loved it. And yet she didn't feel she was a part of it. Didn't feel she should be a part of it.

She didn't fit. She wasn't perfect. She thought she never would be.

I watched her graceful and childlike body disappear before me.
I watched that beautiful girl descend into skeletal madness.

I tried encouraging her to eat while she was in my office.
Light snacks while we talked. I thought that she wouldn't notice she was eating if I distracted her.

She was thin, not stupid.

As she'd leave my office she'd glance sideways at the mirror and I saw the twisted look of terror flash swiftly across her features before she regained her composure and promised me to be "a good girl".

Her smile could melt a thousand hearts.
It melted mine.

I covered the mirror.
I knew she was retching every last morsel of food from her wasted body as soon as she reached her bathroom.

The College doctor came to see me.
Her parents came to see me.
Her friends came to see me.
She was loved. She was adored. She was cherished. She was worried about.
She hated herself.

"I'm fat."

"You're not."

"How can you say that? Look at me."

"You're beautiful."

"I'm not."

"You'll die."

"Maybe."

"Why are you doing this?"

"Because I want to be perfect."

"I can help you see that you're perfect already."

"No you can't, because I'm not."

We argued. We debated.

I grew desperate.

She grew thinner.

And then, one cold autumn day, she stopped coming.

At her funeral I found out that her sister had died ten years earlier from cancer, her small body blown up from drugs and steroids and all the terrible chemicals you push into a child in desperation, to make it live, and then decimated in the last few months until she'd disappeared into nothing.

I found out that she had adored her sister. Worshipped her sister. Missed her sister.

I looked at my own daughter and the cold finger of fear crept into my heart.

She was young, happy and carefree.

Would one day a tragic turning point in her life mean that everything I'd ever taught her, everything my husband had ever taught her, about herself; about life; about happiness; mean nothing?

Would she choose not to talk to me, as Lucy had done? To cut herself off from everyone who loved and cared for her? I held her close and willed her to love herself. As she was.

As I stared at the photo frame atop the coffin at her funeral, the muffled sound of crying filling the church, I realised that this had to be a turning point for me.

I realised that I owed it to Lucy to make sure that no one else believed that they truly needed to destroy their bodies in the pursuit of perfection.

I had to make her tragic mistake count for something and not be a waste of her life.

I knew I had to convince others who came to me, as she had, that life wasn't about perfection. It was about living. Just as we are.

And just as I knew the battle would be hard, I knew somehow that her story might just be the catalyst for change in others.

I knew that I owed it to her sister, who had fought to stay alive and yet had, unknowingly, influenced Lucy to destroy herself.

I took my daughter's hand and walked from the church.

As we passed the coffin I knew Lucy would be watching us.

And nodding her approval.

Reach Inside

Tessa moved from self-loathing to
acceptance of who she was.
And she did it all with the help
of a complete stranger.

My mum always told me that I was chubby.

I still remember the smell of her as I snuggled up on her lap and waited for her hand to rest gently on my head and stroke my hair.

It was a strange smell. A mixture of cigarettes, booze and cheap perfume.

But I loved her.

And I wanted reassurance, even as a small child, that who I am was accepted and cherished by the one person in my life I trusted.

But as I snuggled into her arms her reassurances were always double edged. Yes, she accepted and loved me. She told me she adored me. But she always had to add something into the mix. A comment. An observation. Something wrong about me. Something I felt I had no control over.

My weight.

I know it's easy to say I did have control. But what seven year-old or eleven year-old growing up in a one-parent family has control over what is put on the table?

Mum struggled to put food on the table as well as drink in her glass and the cigarettes which she chain-smoked habitually. The food we ate was simple, plain and filling.

It was also fattening.

It took me until I was fifteen to work out that my mum's criticisms of me were her safety net. That she did her best. But felt that her best wasn't good enough. So she wanted me to need her. Want her reassurances. Believe that I needed to go to her to feel better about myself. That adding that one doubt to my mind about my own perfection kept me a prisoner tied to her apron strings.

And it did.

And then my mum passed away.

I was twenty. She was so young really. But a lifetime of drinking her sorrows away and chain smoking had taken its toll.

The end was bitter, pain-ridden and there was such anger.
From both of us.

She, at dying so early.

Me, at her for leaving me. Abandoning me just as I was about to experience life.

At her bedside I waited for something from her.

A release.

A final reassurance.

That she'd been lying to me all these years. That I really was perfect and that she had kept back from telling me. Let me strive for better things. That she'd done it for my own good.

I got nothing.

She did pat my hand and whisper, *"Good luck kid."*

I gripped her hand tightly. Despite the fact that she'd destroyed my confidence across those years, she'd done the best she could. She'd loved me and put food on the table. But with no partner and a child to bring up it had all been too much.

I felt abandoned. My comfort blanket gone.

I also felt a strange sense of freedom.

But it was too late.

I'd love to say that breaking free was a cathartic experience. It wasn't. In many ways it was terrifying and lonely.
I determined to change my ways. Stop eating for comfort. Hit the gym and exercise my weight into oblivion. Prove to my mum that I could be different. Prove her wrong. Feel better about the new me.

The free me.

But the doubts sown over two decades had taken root and were expanding, seeking further sources of nutrition to feed them.

And the weight that was the testament to two decades of self-doubt and self-humiliation and aching need never shifted.

But I've finally reached a point in my life where I've accepted who I am.

Embraced myself and given myself that virtual hug I should have done years ago.

The hug that is unconditional. With no barbed comments at the back of it. I've also patted myself gently on the back and reassured myself.

That it's okay to be me. Nothing more. Certainly nothing less.

That what the world thought. Still thinks. About me. Didn't matter. Doesn't matter.

I realised that the beauty that only some can see is hidden behind this mask.

This outer shell. And I've come to see the mask I wear, my size and shape, as useful.

And beautiful and wondrous.

That to find out the true essence of someone you have to put out a hand and reach inside to make that discovery.

Like the cover of a book. The real story is in the pages inside, not on the cover.

The cover can be misleading. It can look colourful, attractive, exciting.

But inside the story can be dull, uninteresting, easily forgotten.

On the other hand a simple, bland cover can hide a story which can keep you up at night, turning page after page, desperate to find out more, devouring the entire contents until you breathlessly reach the end and ache for more.

I'm that simple brown cover. Boring to look at. Certainly not physically attractive. But open the cover and delve inside and you'd be surprised, amazed, entranced.

I saw someone one day.

Unexpectedly.

One of those ships that pass your bow briefly, never to be seen again.

Someone whom I've never laid eyes on since. And she was my turning point.

My smack upside the head.

I was on the bus. Coming back from an exhausting day at the office. Reading the newspaper I'd grabbed in the morning and had stuffed in my bag to read later.

A shadow cut the light from the view of my paper and I looked up, irritated that the lights might have gone out.

But the lights were still on.

Moving through the bus was a woman.

She was huge.

Massive.

I watched as some of my fellow passengers glanced up at her and looked away again, embarrassment written all over their faces.

In a single second they judged what they'd seen and dismissed it.

I guessed that a whole lot of them made themselves feel good because of it. Because it wasn't them. Perhaps some felt sympathy. Or even loathing. Then they mentally moved on.

I didn't.

For a single moment I fought the feeling of fascination and hurriedly raised my paper.

My thoughts raced. I mustn't stare. I don't usually stare at anyone. Did people stare at me like this and I never realised it? I felt a scarlet blush crawl up my skin and hoped no one saw.

But I couldn't help myself.

She might be huge, but she was so graceful.

Her dress, a billowing tent surrounding her frame.
And yet she glided almost, as she moved. A skater on ice.

Her head was held high as she looked for a vacant seat.

I found myself engrossed in fascination.

She was elegant and proud in a way that surprised me. Certainly I'd never felt elegant or proud about myself. I usually moved fast and awkwardly to get out of people's sight as quickly as I could.

She was an enigma to me.
She manoeuvred to sit across two seats in front of me.

I glanced at the irritated look on the passenger's face the other side of her. Irritation that she was intruding on more than one seat. Something I do all the time and feel embarrassed about myself. Invading more space than I'm entitled to.

But she didn't look embarrassed.

I caught the look of contempt cross the man's features as he shook his head and raised his newspaper noisily.

Trying to make her feel guilty.

Trying to make her feel bad about herself.

I felt a sudden wave of understanding for the woman flush my system. And embarrassment at the callousness of my fellow passenger.

I peeked from behind my newspaper and noticed how confident she was as she settled down and took out her book.

I realised as I gazed back at my newspaper that I admired her. I envied her.

And then, when I hoped no one was looking, I glanced at her face.

Her eyes.

In that single second I caught sight of the beauty behind the eyes.

The kindness.
The compassion.
The humanity.
The sheer elegance in her face.

I fought the desire to reach across and speak to her. It would be inappropriate.

But I'd like to have done it. And I regret that I didn't to this day.

I'd like to have told her I thought she was beautiful. I'd like to have said sorry for the man's ignorance and rudeness.

But I didn't.

I didn't have the courage, or the audacity, or the confidence.

And yet I knew that she was beautiful and something told me she knew it too.

But I knew that what I'd done was the turning point for me.

I'd reached inside and found the truth. I'd penetrated the shell surrounding that woman and saw her heart and her soul.

And I understood.

And I knew that despite what I felt about myself, perhaps others saw me differently.

That they too looked at me and reached across, and penetrated my shell and saw the real me.

You know, one day I might just progress from being that brown covered book that looks dull and uninteresting and hides the exciting story inside.

One day I'm going to be a Best Seller.

Mirror Mirror

Can a piece of glass really hold that much power over how we feel about ourselves?

It never ceases to amaze me.

I can feel fantastic about myself.

Revel in my new outfit, touch up my make up and run a comb through my beautifully styled hair and then it happens.

It's so predictable as to be laughable and you'd think I would be used to it by now.

But I'm not and it takes me by surprise every time.

With regular monotony.

I turn to go out of the bedroom and there it is.

The full-length mirror.

Every girl's supposed best friend, but in reality, every girl's worst nightmare.

Because it's there that I stop. Transfixed by the reality.

The image in front of my face isn't the one I imagined.

It's certainly not the confident person who turned seconds ago from the dressing table and strode towards the bedroom door.

It's the real me.

The imperfect vision I was trying to hide from the world.

The person I never imagine I am, but always greets me as I get ready to face my critics and the world outside, my friends and family.

In a single blow from a simple pane of glass framed in teak, my self-esteem plummets and no matter what my husband says, no matter what confidence-building praise I get from the children or my friends in the next few hours, the image remains.

The real deal.

Unattractive, overweight and not particularly special.

No matter what I've dressed myself up in, the mirror reveals everything I don't want it to and more.

There they are.
The bulges which I've tried to disguise with clothes or jewellery draped seductively across my breasts.

This in a vain attempt to throw the onlooker off the scent.

From looking further down and seeing the love handles bulging unattractively or the padded midriff not in the slightest restrained by the newest line in "hold-em-in" underwear.

Underwear, I'll have you know, which cost me so much money, I almost gasped at the cash desk as I hurriedly paid for them in embarrassment.
I really hoped the women behind me hadn't glimpsed my purchase.
I really hoped that they didn't realise what the assistant was pushing neatly into a bag.

Of course, I knew in my heart that if I turned around they'd be the image of perfection and would look disdainfully at the poor wretch in front of them helplessly forced into buying the newest line in support panties.

You know that feeling don't you?

As I pause, eyeing the mirror suspiciously - as I always do - running my hands down my outfit to smooth out any potential creases, any potential for eye-catching imperfection, I catch sight of a skin blemish.

In reality if I'm truthful there's usually more than one, it just depends on which one has made it first through the layer of foundation I've nicely plastered over my face.

You see, what's reflected back at me from that mirror is reality. It's the Me they see. It's just that it's not the Me I expect to see. Not the Me I imagine I am or look like, and it's a nasty surprise.

Am I really that fat?

Does my double chin always have to look so pronounced?
Perhaps if I tip my head backwards it'll disappear. Nope. It's still there.

I'm shorter than I always imagine.
Even with those lovely heels I strapped my feet into, I'm still stumpy.

I guess if I look full on at myself, things aren't so bad, but turn sideways, even for a second and every lump, bump and unwanted curve is there.

I'd thought my hair was just perfect. Now it's not looking how I thought it looked.
I flick a hairbrush through it hurriedly, for the third time since I got up from the chair.

I can't tell you how many times I've sighed and deflated like a balloon on seeing my reflection.

I should take the mirror away.

Banish it to some dark corner in the guest room where only my guests can suffer the humiliation of the reflected glory.

But we girls all need to at least see if we're hitched up right, not displaying some embarrassing tucked piece of skirt into our panties or our petticoat isn't a half an inch too long. Too long for that lovely knee length silk piece of fabric that looked so delightful on the rail in the shop but showed a little more than we wanted it to when we got it on, and the sun cheekily revealed legs reaching up higher than we knew we had.

Oh boy!

So the mirror stays.

A necessary evil and a window onto everything we thought we weren't.
Everything we pretend we're not like.

Because without the reflection we can imagine we are more perfect than we are.
Thinner, more curvy, more attractive, taller, shorter.
More anything.

I've tried glancing quickly as I go past. Maybe if I look and look away again really fast my glance will reveal what I want it to.

It never works. A glance turns into a long stare. I'm doomed to hate my reflection.

It reminds me of the fairy story where the Queen continually asked her mirror who was the most beautiful of all and it told her every day that she was.

My mirror doesn't tell such porky pies.

It's truthful and honest and straight with me. It tells it like it is.

What it can't reveal is what's inside me.

What's behind those eyes, which look tentatively at the outside world and hide the essence that I am.

The heart, the soul and the mind.

The love I feel.

The kindness of my nature.

The mother, sister, wife, daughter, friend or simply the person that I really am.

So a mirror can't show everything there is about us.

That has to be left to the person who looks at you, who makes eye contact and can catch a glimpse of the soul behind the face, behind the imperfect body, behind the physical you.

Even if you smile at your reflection and it smiles back, it can't reveal the feelings and the warmth behind the smile.

It's just a piece of glass.

It takes a human, another soul to delve deeply and discover the essence of a person.

My mirror will never reflect me.

It will always just reflect the shell surrounding the real me.

It's not magic. If it was, when I said *"Mirror, mirror who is the most beautiful of all?"* it might just come back with an answer I'd like.

For the moment this mere mortal will just have to go on glancing and hoping that the image I see isn't actually the image everyone else is seeing.

Because true beauty can only be seen through another human pair of eyes and my mirror definitely isn't human.

Elation

Perhaps Sasha's belief that the darkest
hour is just before dawn will surprise
you and make you think

I'm glad you've stopped in. I've got some news.

Sit down for a while and talk to me.

I want you to think about something.

What do you think is the worst thing that someone can tell you?

No really. The worst thing.
What do you dread most in life?

It's hard isn't it?

The fact is I'm guessing you're thinking about one thing.

I dread being told I've got cancer or some life threatening disease.

In fact, dig deeper and you'll realise that it's not the worst thing you
can be told.
There is something far worse.

Well, there is to me anyway.
But I'll get to that.

I know you weren't expecting this but you see, I'm very sick.

I know. I'm sorry to have to tell you.
But you probably wouldn't notice at the moment.

Not unless you really stared at my face and analysed the dark circles
under my eyes or the weird colour of my skin right now.

See it now?

Yes, that's right. I know. It's subtle.
So are the rest of the changes that are going on.
At least on the outside.
For the moment it's all hidden.

A cancer eating away at my insides. Secretly.

My secret. Well, mine and the doctor at the hospital knows, and a
very few close members of my immediate family, and I wanted to
tell you as well.

So now you know.

And it's a secret which is making me feel so tired.
So unwell, I never thought I could ever feel this bad.
So worn out.

Yet.

So relieved.

So determined.

So optimistic.

So elated.

Does that sound strange to you?
That I should feel relieved or elated?
Optimistic even?

You look stunned that I should say that.
Well, let me explain.

Once you've got over the initial shock of being told your life is about
to change.

That things you took for granted just might not be around for much
longer.
That you can stop thinking of the future as a given.
Stop dreaming about tomorrow and concentrate on today.
Once you've got over all of that.

And the tears stop flowing.
And the phone stops ringing.
And you stop having to explain to people.
And people get used to the idea.
And the looks of sympathy stop.
And you get back to your life and what's about to happen in it.

Then you start to realise that the worst thing most people think you
could ever be told has just happened.
That thing everyone dreads.
The big C.

And you're still standing.
And still loving.
And still hoping.
And still embracing life.

So yes, I'm relieved.
I can move forward now.
There's nothing else to dread.
At least not about me personally.

I remember telling my doctor, when he delivered the news, that in
fact the worst thing someone can be told is that a close relative or
best friend has cancer. Not yourself.

He seemed surprised.

Are you?
Really? Seriously?

Have a think about it.

Handle your own sickness and your own destiny and cope with it, or watch someone you love so much it hurts, fight the fight you want to fight for them and can't.

Is it selfish to prefer to be the one to take up the sword and fight?
Perhaps.
But that's for another time.
We can have another conversation.
Sometime in the future.

And let me tell you.
For me it's not all pessimism.
It's not all dark thoughts and misery.
That word you're wondering how I'm feeling it.

Elation.

I'm elated because I realise that whatever happens to me now physically, they can't touch what's on the inside.

And I've reached a peace.
And it's beautiful.
And it's wonderful.
Because I've always been wrapped up in the outer me.
My image.

What everyone thought about me.
What I looked like.
What my hair looked like.

Well, soon they tell me I won't have any to worry about.
And I can buy a wig in any style or colour I like.
Or look incredibly trendy and wrap a scarf tightly around my head
and imagine I'm someone deliciously chic.

I always bothered whether my make up was perfect.
Well, the dark circles under my eyes are soon going to be increasingly difficult to disguise.

And why worry about them now?
Why disguise them?
I have more important things to do.

I always dieted and worried about how fat I am.
Well that's about to change, so they say.

I remember my sister in law.
God bless her.
I loved her so much.
She was diagnosed with cancer and we went shopping.
She was 40.
She'd always considered herself to be chunky and a big girl.

I just loved her unconditionally and saw her as perfect.
She'd lost a lot of weight suddenly. Heaps. She went down about
three sizes.
We hit this lovely boutique in Carnaby Street in London.
She put on this lovely dress. It hung beautifully. She looked stunning.

I remember the radiance in her face. She simply smiled at me and
said.

*"I've finally got to the size I wanted to be all my life. And it feels so
good."*

I remember hugging her tight.
We laughed together a lot that day.
It was the last time we went shopping.

She is my role model.
She made good come out of tragedy.
She lived life to the full.
Right up until she died.
She was one of the most beautiful women I ever knew.

So, no.
I'm not going to moan about what's happening.
Or spend my time dwelling on how crap the cards were dealt.
I'm going to live it.
Accept it.

Be grateful it's me and not one of my family or closest friends.
Embrace the changes as best I can.
Work with my body.
Tend to it.
Love it.
Soothe it.

Help it go through what it has to go through.

Learn what I should have learned at least thirty years ago.
That there's so much more to us than what we look like.
What we wear.
What people think about our appearance.

Life's not a rehearsal.
You've just got to live it.

Tube Lines

As we age, what changes? Us? Or merely the perception of us?

You know I've often stared at the Tube map that is outside the Underground station down the street. The lines travelling from left to right, up and down. Some thicker than others. Different colours. I can't see it clearly nowadays but I remember it well enough to fill in the gaps that are blurred.

I know it's a strange preoccupation. But hear me out.

Those lines. They all have a beginning and they all have an end. Some cross others. Crossroads where the lines pause at a station, blend together for a moment and then rush away in the direction they were meant to take. The end of the line, their destiny. They can't alter it. There's no scope because the map is already written. Hand crafted by its maker.

And then I've peered hard at my face in the mirror when I arrive back at my little terraced house.

I can't help smiling as I've unwound the warm winter scarf from my neck, and I've found myself nodding at my reflection.

Those lines I've seen somewhere else. In fact for some long time now I've seen them every day. They've become a part of me. Of who I am.

They're the wrinkles and the furrows which so gracefully inhabit my reflection and when I look away, I catch sight of, running the length of my hands and across my fingers, gnarled now with arthritis and painfully bent out of shape.

I can see you sitting there and thinking;

Just another old woman moaning about how wrinkled her skin has got and how things aren't what they used to be. Listen to her.

But that's where you're wrong. I'm not moaning. I'm rejoicing in them. I'm proud of every single one of them. I'm proud of what they speak about.

They tell a story that would knock your socks off if you stopped and took the time to listen. They're the story of my life and they're engraved on my face and in my body so that I never forget.

Never forget my mother's arms wrapped around me when I was tiny and scared.

Never forget my first kiss.

Never forget the worries.

Never forget the joys.

Never forget the loves I've had.

Never forget the friends who've journeyed with me but sadly departed this world before me.

Never forget walking down that aisle on my father's arm.

Never forget giving birth to my first child.

Never forget losing him hours later, cradled in my arms.

Never forget climbing a mountain so high it took my breath away.

Never forget standing on the side of a fjord in Norway and watching the Northern Lights dance across the sky.

The list is so long, sometimes I just sit down and let my mind wander back and I sink into the moment and experience it again.

If it's a sad memory then I let the tears fall down these wrinkled old cheeks and I feel better for it.

If it's funny then it makes me laugh. Out loud sometimes.

My old cat looks at me suspiciously then.

You see every one of these wrinkles and bent fingers and gnarled joints was hard won. Fought for. Trophies.
Along with the grey hair.
Along with the sagging body parts.
Along with the loss of hair in areas I used to moan about shaving, and now wished I had to do.

Along with the deafness, which means I can't always hear what you're saying.

Along with the blindness in my one eye which makes me squint at you and give you those funny looks you say old ladies always seem to give.

You see, beneath the old wrinkled exterior, and the drying skin and the lines and the greyness and the funny looks, there's me.

Me. A woman.
I don't feel any different to you.
Not deep inside.
Not in my mind.
Not in the way I think.

I still dance to music even though I can't move around the room without my stick. I close my eyes and I let my mind take me onto the dance floor and let the music rush through my veins and in my heart I'm free to move. And the music sends my spirits soaring.

And I still enjoy films, and yes, as surprising as it may seem I still fall in love with the hero and envy the heroine. They might be only as old as my grandchildren are but in this young mind I can dream that I'm young again and can fall in love. Just like the rest of you.

I was like you once.

Physically that is.

Young, energetic, smooth skinned, hearing everything, seeing all and pushing a hand through thick locks of glossy red hair, and strutting my stuff, proud and tall and beautiful.

And all you see now is a small, bent over old woman. You don't see me as beautiful. Do you?

But look again.

And try to imagine those trophy lines swept away, and those eyes, both of them wide open and deep blue, not with that opacity that my old age has glazed across them.

Try to imagine my hair thicker and redder and my lips open and fuller. My hands slender with beautifully manicured nails and feet, which stood flat and firm.

I ask you to try and imagine it, because if you do you will see my beauty.

Because I know that when you look at me now you can't see it.

You don't see the beauty behind the face.

But it's there.

And I'm proud of all the years that have swept away the surface, and all the battles I've fought and all the battles I've won.

I'm proud of all the people whose lives I've affected and made better.

I'm proud of all the hands I've taken and walked beside through the trials of life.

And I'm proud of something else.

I'm proud of me.

Reflections

Our friends are reflections of what we are.
Pieces of glass in which we see ourselves,
our humanity, and our self-worth.

She is my friend.
I don't say that lightly.
Or falsely.
It means something. A lot.
That word.
Friend.

It means that we have chosen each other.
She and I.
From all those people out there.
That she and I connect in some way.
Understand each other.
Find each other beautiful.
Inside.

She's compassionate, loving, wise.
She also says that about me.
She's fun and modest and full of depth.
I make her laugh. And cry.

I can tell her my deepest thoughts.
I can share my inner feelings.
My guilty secrets. My worries.
I can confess to her.
In safety.

We can talk together.
Drink together.
Eat together.
Shop together.
Laugh together.
Cry together.

She shares her world with me.
Allows me into her life.
Trusts me.
Opens her heart.
And knows it won't get broken.

The paths we walked separately from birth
Converged briefly when we met
And gave us a chance to decide
Whether we wanted to continue along the new one
As friends.
And we did.

There are categories.
Of friends.
Best friends, close friends, social friends, workplace friends,
family friends.

Some stay only briefly. A few years perhaps.
Others remain in our hearts forever.
If we're lucky.

If we're unlucky, some disappoint us.
Hurt us. Betray our trust.
And then we realise they weren't really friends at all.
Ever.
Because they didn't really fit the word "friend".
Did they?

Because friends don't hurt us. Can't hurt us.
They wouldn't want to. Or need to.

But this is a real friendship.
And it's not possible to stop being her friend.
If I did that then I'd lose a part of me.

Of who I am.
Of what I mean to this world.
Because being her friend has become part of my life.
My reflection.

Our friends make us who we are.
What we feel.
How we treat people.
Become a part of our humanity
And a reason for our compassion.

By loving my friend
I have to love myself
Because she can't love someone who isn't beautiful,
Because she is.
Perhaps that should be one of the universal laws?

I think this one already is.
Friendship matters.
A lot.

About the Author

British writer Julia Hague was born in London, UK in 1957 and grew up with the Beatles and all things swinging sixties-wise around her. An avid writer from a very early age she has written from her teens through to the present day. Living her entire life in London, she says, has provided her with a unique backdrop of culture, diversity and richness in which to develop and grow, both as a human being and as an observer of life and the people who inhabit it.

"I'm fascinated by people and I love them. How they react with one another. How they treat one another. How they grow and how they live. What they feel about themselves and the others around them. I've always said that life is about the people in it, not what you have. Without people to interact with, to love, to cherish and to care for, we're just one-dimensional. Just sit in a pavement café and observe what happens around you. It's more interesting than anything on the television. People can be wonderfully compassionate and caring and have this amazing capacity for love and for making those around them feel good. At the same time they can be cruel, heartless and selfish. We're unique and worthy of respect and love. And we each possess beauty. That's each of us. We just have to realise it and see it in others. And more importantly, embrace it."

Julia is happily married with a grown-up daughter and still lives in the city which gives her so much creative food for thought. She juggles a full-time career as a Personal Assistant, with being the Chairman of an Events Company and writing poetry, plays, science fiction, biographical material and song lyrics in whatever spare time she finds.

—m—

CREDITS

Lightning Source UK Ltd.
Milton Keynes UK
12 December 2009

147407UK00001B/207/P